Behind The Scenes In
SOCIAL SECURITY

Vanessa Ann Bates

Copyright © 2023 **Van Bates Publishing**

All rights reserved. No part of this publication may be reproduced, distributed, or transmitted in any form or by any means, including photocopying, recording, or other electronic or mechanical methods, without the prior written permission of the publisher, except in the case of brief quotations embodied in critical reviews and certain other noncommercial uses permitted by copyright law. For permission requests, write to the publisher, addressed "Attention: Book Rights and Permission," at the address below.

Published in the United States of America

ISBN 978-1-962110-89-1 (SC)
ISBN 978-1-962110-88-4 (Ebook)

Van Bates Publishing
1901 Amanda Ct,
Upper Marlboro, MD 20774
www.vanessabates.com/

Order Information and Rights Permission:

Quantity sales. Special discounts might be available on quantity purchases by corporations, associations, and others. For details, contact the publisher at the address above.

For Book Rights Adaptation and other Rights Permission. Call us at toll-free 1-888-945-8513 or send us an email at admin@stellarliterary.com

Contents

Summary iv
Dedication v

Chapter 1   The Beneficiaries Who Could Not Read 1
Chapter 2   Mentally Ill Beneficiaries 2
Chapter 3   The Little Girl That Suffered Incest 4
Chapter 4   Office Personnel Management: Beneficiary Tax Problem 5
Chapter 5   Beneficiary Losing a Million-Dollar Home 6
Chapter 6   Beneficiary Losing Life Over $40 8
Chapter 7   The Apartheid 10
Chapter 8   The Preacher Whose Taxes Were Filed Wrong 11
Chapter 9   Children Fighting The Parents Over Their Benefits 13
Chapter 10 True Love 15
Chapter 11 Adventures In The Field 17
Chapter 12 Heady Supervisors 19
Chapter 13 The Power of God 21
Chapter 14 Senior Citizen Wanted to Be Young 23
Chapter 15 The Disobedient Child 25
Chapter 16 Deformed Claimant 27
Chapter 17 I Hurt My Butt On The Front Desk 29
Chapter 18 The Drunk 30
Chapter 19 Dealing With Ex Convicts 31
Chapter 20 A Note to The Millennials 33
Chapter 21 My Gift To The United States Citizens 35
Chapter 22 An Innocent Girl 36
Chapter 23 How to get a claim 38
Chapter 24 Compassion 40
Chapter 25 Helped All Mankind But Could Not Help My Father 42
Chapter 26 The Cancer Victim 44
Chapter 27 The Little Girl Who Found Hope 46
Chapter 28 The Man Who Had No Teeth 47
Chapter 29 The Prophesy 49
Chapter 30 Is Social Security Going Broke? 51

About The Author 55

SUMMARY

Are you wondering what happens behind the scenes at the Social Security office? This fascinating book takes you on a journey through the adventures of an employee working for the agency. From heart-wrenching stories of seniors struggling with lack and hardship to hilarious encounters with humor-filled senior citizens, this book will leave you laughing and empathizing with the tales shared within. If you're looking for a riveting read full of insight and emotion, this book is for you. Don't miss out on the opportunity to gain a deeper understanding of what takes place in the world of social security. Get your hands on this page-turner today!

DEDICATION

I dedicate this book to my late father, John Bates Sr. John worked his entire life doing hard labor in hopes that one day someone would take care of him and he would receive his retirement benefits. John, my father, had to work from age seven to seventy because he was left an orphan, and the people that took him in made him work for a living. No schooling for him! With a first-grade education, he overcame life challenges and became self-employed.

Because the laws read, at that time, and tend to return, if a person owns his own business, he cannot retire until age 70. Also, unless he gives up his business, he cannot receive disability, whether dying of cancer or not. How unfair!

I'm sorry, DAD, that I could not change Congress' laws. Hopefully, Jesus is taking care of you now. May you rest in peace.

Love,
Your Daughter and Family

CHAPTER 1
THE BENEFICIARIES WHO COULD NOT READ

It was just another regular day at the Social Security Office until two rough-and-tumble fellows strutted in, looking for a replacement card. As I explained the application process, they sheepishly admitted, "Ma'am, we can't read during the day. We went to night school!" Their lighthearted joke belied the sad reality that many individuals from the baby boomer era could not read or write.

Not wanting to deny them their rights, I stepped up and filled out the application on their behalf. It was a small gesture, but it made a big difference in their lives. It reminded me how important it is to provide accessible services to everyone, regardless of their literacy level; and who knows, maybe one day those two fellas will return as successful business owners or learned scholars, all thanks to a little assistance from a government worker.

CHAPTER 2
MENTALLY ILL BENEFICIARIES

One day, I was working at the social security office when a mentally ill person approached me for assistance. The lobby was packed with people, and I tried my best to help, but suddenly the situation turned violent. The person pulled out a knife and knocked my computer off the counter, missing my feet by just inches.

Thankfully, a security guard quickly jumped into action and wrestled the individual to the ground. It was a difficult struggle as mentally ill people can have surprisingly strong physical abilities. In a panic, I ran for safety while the guard heroically managed to apprehend the perpetrator and confiscate the knife. A sarcastic employee asked me, "What did you do in the commotion?" I looked at him and said, "I said to my feet, "'Feet, don't fail me now!'""

This was not an isolated incident. Many individuals with mental disabilities would come into our office, and sometimes things would turn violent. In fact, I even advised the security guard to hide her stick as a weapon in case someone used it against us.

These violent encounters occurred frequently, especially as most offices were in rough neighborhoods. Unfortunately, when things got out of hand, the police often wouldn't show up. Working at the social security office was challenging and sometimes dangerous, and I witnessed many heartbreaking situations. These are just a few stories that left a lasting impact on me.

CHAPTER 3
THE LITTLE GIRL THAT SUFFERED INCEST

As I sat in my office, a nervous mother walked in with her two children. I couldn't help but notice the little girl who seemed around five years old but had a mature haircut.

Curiosity got the better of me, and I asked the mother why she gave her baby girl such a grown-up hairstyle. What followed next broke my heart. The mother confided in me that her family was suffering from a sinister issue- incest.

My heart sank, and I could see the despair in her eyes. The poor little girl was so scared of her father that she feared her hair would fall out. To top it off, the father tracked them using their social security number and wanted to indulge in horrendous acts with his own flesh and blood.

After calming the mother down, I decided to take matters into my own hands. I researched the program manual and found a way to assign a new social security number under the police request for identity protection. I felt that divine intervention led me to this pivotal moment, and I could make a difference in this family's life.

I'm happy to say that this family now has a fresh start. My heart aches when I think of what they've been through, but I'm proud I could help.

CHAPTER 4
OFFICE PERSONNEL MANAGEMENT: BENEFICIARY TAX PROBLEM

An elderly couple in dire need approached me for assistance. They had just been evicted from their home due to unpaid taxes on their federal government pension. They had no idea they were liable to pay taxes on their retirement and, unfortunately, exceeded the three-year limit. This left them with a hefty tax bill they couldn't afford to pay in full.

Without hesitation, I contacted a liaison for their congressmen to see if there was any way to mitigate their situation. Fortunately, we were able to come up with a solution: they could pay the taxes in installments. Thanks to some divine intervention, God is Good: the couple was able to return to their beloved home without losing it.

This story serves as a reminder that sometimes, life can be unpredictable, and we could all use a helping hand at some point. As a community, we need to offer support and guidance to those who need it most, especially our elderly population, who often lack the resources and knowledge. Let's continue to show kindness and compassion to one another, as we never know when we may need it in return.

CHAPTER 5
BENEFICIARY LOSING A MILLION-DOLLAR HOME

Once upon a time, there was an elderly woman who was on the verge of losing her home. She had worked hard for years to own a house in Georgetown and had almost paid it off with just three thousand dollars left. However, a sudden turn of events threw her entire world into chaos. Her bank, where she had arranged for her mortgage to be paid from her direct deposit of social security payment, went out of business! Due to this, her payments were lost, and she found herself with only three hours to pay the mortgage or risk losing her precious home.

To make matters worse, the bank where her social security benefits were deposited closed down, too, causing her payments to be returned to social security and suspended. They could only resume when they found a better address to send payments to, but that took over a year! It was a time of great turmoil as many banks closed in the early 90s, and beneficiaries struggled to find new places to receive their payments.

One day, while reviewing the information on the computer, I discovered that the lady's payments were in suspense at the agency. But time was of the essence, and we only had three hours! So, I quickly alerted the computer that I was issuing a critical payment to the lady and paying her mortgage with her suspended benefits. It was a race against time, but we managed to release the payment just in time, and she was able to keep her home.

The moral of the story is that even in times of crisis, there are people who care and are willing to go the extra mile to help those in need. It may take some time and effort, but never give up hope, for there is always a solution to every problem.

CHAPTER 6
BENEFICIARY LOSING LIFE OVER $40

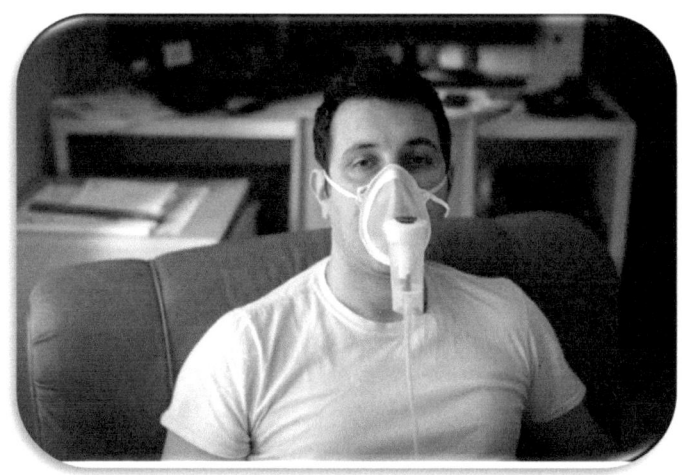

In a quiet, unassuming office, an unlikely figure shuffled in. His unkempt appearance and rough edges did not inspire confidence among the employees, who avoided helping him. However, as fate would have it, I was the one to whom he made his desperate appeal.

"Ma'am," he began, voice choking with emotion," I'm going to lose my life over just forty dollars. Nobody in my life has that much to spare. The electricity company is cutting me off, and I depend on my respirator to survive. If they terminate the service, I'll die."

Moved by his heartbreaking story, I delved into his records, determined to find a solution. It was then that I discovered that the agency owed him exactly forty dollars which he desperately needed. He was on Medicare, and though they had paid his bill, the payment was stuck in limbo, taking thirty long days to process.

I immediately contacted the electric company, explaining the critical nature of the situation. I pleaded with them to give me just two days to issue the much-needed payment, as it was after business hours. The possibility of the man losing his life over such a small amount was too much to bear.

The next day, he returned, and I quickly alerted headquarters through the computer that a critical payment of forty dollars needed to be made to save his precious life. The payment was issued, and the electric company continued to provide services. His life was saved, all thanks to a little bit of kindness and quick thinking.

CHAPTER 7
THE APARTHEID

You won't be able to hold back tears after reading about this inspiring woman's story. She was a stunning and bright lady who walked into the social security office seeking aid to get benefits. It had been a decade since her husband passed away in the dreadful era of apartheid in Africa, and the country was still struggling to catch up. It took her five years to receive her husband's death certificate! She shared that she was an American citizen from New Jersey, and her husband was African. After her husband's death, she brought her two kids back to America.

She then went to the American Embassy and filed a claim for benefits. My heart skipped a beat when I checked the computer and found out that we owed her a massive sum of $64,000.00 in back benefits! I wrote to the Social Security International Affairs Department to release the payment. Finally, after just thirty days, the lady showed up in our office, thrilled to report that she had indeed received payment and now has a house to call home.

Thanks to the huge sum she received, she and her children no longer have to experience the abuse and torture of apartheid. Back in those days, they were mistreated merely because of their skin color, but now they've found a place where they can finally be truly free—America, the land of liberty, freedom no matter what race, gender, or culture.

CHAPTER 8
THE PREACHER WHOSE TAXES WERE FILED WRONG

As the minister entered my office to file for retirement at the age of sixty-five, little did I know what was about to unfold. Upon bringing up his earnings, I was dismayed to find that there were none. No earnings at all! I searched high and low but could find no record of his income. I double-checked to see if they had been filed under the wrong number, but still, there was nothing.

The only other explanation was that the minister's taxes were filed incorrectly. As I went over the returns with a fine-tooth comb, the minister's accountant screamed and yelled so loudly that his spat got all over me, making me faint! The lesson about banks keeping the money was dropped. The accountant had forgotten to attach the tax form 941SE to the minister's federal taxes to pay his social security taxes. This was an accounting error that caused the minister to lose his retirement. I informed the minister that this error had effectively destroyed his retirement.

The minister was understandably upset, though it was the accountant's fault. Unfortunately, the accountant refused to admit his mistake. He got in my face, spitting and screaming, causing me to feel faint and weak. Praying to God to keep me conscious, I bore the brunt of the accountant's anger. It was a difficult situation, especially given that this was a church matter.

Despite our best efforts, we could not find a way to entitle the minister to benefits without his filing twenty years of amended returns. Due to his unwillingness to do this, we were left with no other options. This was the first time in my career that someone had spat on me, leaving me feeling sick and shaken.

Regardless, I will never forget this situation or the valuable lesson I learned about the importance of filing taxes correctly. It was a poignant reminder that even the smallest of errors can have a significant impact on someone's future.

CHAPTER 9
CHILDREN FIGHTING THE PARENTS OVER THEIR BENEFITS

A liquor store owner came into our office with a perplexing problem involving a beneficiary who had been cashing two checks every month. To get to the bottom of this, I asked him to bring the beneficiary in so we could better understand the situation. And boy, were we in for a shock.

It turns out that when the lady's social security check arrived in the mail, her own daughter would snatch it and use it for herself! And to make matters worse, the lady would then file for a duplicate payment, claiming she never received the original check. It was a domestic dispute that had our jaws dropping in disbelief.

The consequences of this deception were dire. The liquor store owner was at risk of losing his license unless he paid back the overpayment in benefits. At this point, we stepped in to help. We had the lady sign an agreement to pay back the overpayment in installment payments that were feasible for her.

Although the daughter's actions constituted forgery, the lady refused to press charges against her own flesh and blood. Therefore, we had to come up with a solution that would allow the lady's benefits to continue while ensuring the overpayment was paid back in due time.

In the end, justice was served, and lessons were learned. You never know what secrets lie behind closed doors, but with our help, we can help you navigate even the trickiest situations.

CHAPTER 10
TRUE LOVE

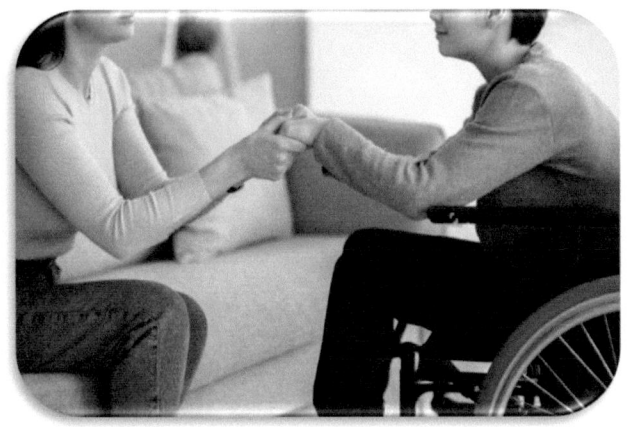

A lady came in needing an award letter for her adopted paraplegic son. The computers were down at the time. I told her I would give her a letter for Medicare to pay his medical bills once the computer came back up. The lady loved her son and wanted him to have medical treatment. She prayed so hard that I was able to give her the letter within an hour. She went on to say the administration had miscalculated his benefits and was going to cut off the little boy's SSI check. She said they had so many expenses that she could not afford to repay them.

I advised them that I would try to have the overpayment waived if she brought in all their bills. I requested a waiver of overpayment, documenting all expenses and proving the mistake was the administration's fault and they could not afford to repay. The waiver was granted!

The little boy went home to be with the Lord. While he had breath, none of his checks were stopped or interrupted, and Heim and his mom never had to repay the missed calculation.

I never knew anyone who loved someone so much. Adopted paraplegic and disabled, you could feel this lady's love for the child in conversation. True love!!!!

In this world of uncertainty and chaos, it's heartening to see that love and kindness still prevail. This story will restore your faith in humanity and remind you that there's always someone out there who cares. True love has no boundaries, whether the person is young, old, pretty, ugly, disabled, healthy, rich, or poor. There is someone who will love you for who or what you are.

CHAPTER 11
ADVENTURES IN THE FIELD

The office would assign positions and tasks outside your job description and classify them under it, using the phrase "other duties as assigned." This prevented any chances of promotion or improved compensation for performing higher-level work.

On many occasions, I ventured out into the field with a colleague to gather information and resolve issues regarding post-entitlement benefits. This was a precarious job, as we acted as field representatives and had to visit impoverished regions in northeast and southeast Washington, D.C.

During one field trip, we encountered a particularly hazardous environment. A building had sewage spilling out of the basement, and rats as large as cats were roaming free. While walking down the street, a man approached me and said, "Boat boat." My partner informed me that he was attempting to sell me LSD acid, but at the time, I thought he was referring to The Love Boat TV show. I later realized my mistake.

The situation escalated as a 4x4 truck drove down the street, with packs of drugs being handed out according to hand signs. People were collecting money based on the number of drugs they requested. We were driving through the area at noon, and it seemed like Mardi Gras with people out on the street. The truck started flinging packs of drugs, and my partner shouted, "Dope, dope!" I quickly drove away.

After that incident, I reported to headquarters that going out into the field was too dangerous and life-threatening for us. From then on, I was no longer required to visit homes in impoverished regions.

CHAPTER 12
HEADY SUPERVISORS

"You know, you can't give power or position to some people as they abuse their power. One day I was in the center of the office, and my supervisor came up to me saying, "I'm your supervisor; I have control over your life. You stop serving God and serve me." Shocked by her audacity, I said, "No, I will not stop serving God, and He will let you know who He is!" In response, she threw a weed on me, which infected my sinus. I had to rush to my doctor's office and take antibiotics.

Sadly, her behavior did not stop there. After my father died from cancer, she would not let me take leave to make funeral arrangements, and when I grieved his death, the stress weakened my immune system, and I came down with the flu. In retaliation, she wrote a report to the Area Director, stating it took me two weeks to start a case, attempting to terminate my position. I did a rebuttal, explaining that I was out sick and had been preparing my father's funeral arrangements. I further noted that if someone's dog died, they would be allowed to grieve their loss, so why not me?

I showed the Area Director my leave request and provided proof that I had been out for the cases she had mentioned. Needless to say, the Area Director put her in another office. This experience taught me never to underestimate the power of God. You may be up today and down tomorrow, so treat people with kindness and respect at all times. They did not know God was planning an escape for me to have my own business and refrain from mistreating employees. Instead, I pray for them when they are sick or grieving a misfortune or loss. Giving them hope is essential and not depriving them of their faith in God."

CHAPTER 13
THE POWER OF GOD

It was just an ordinary day when an illegal alien walked into my office, seeking a social security card. As a responsible citizen, I documented the case and made copies of the false identification he provided. Little did I know that it would lead to a life-changing event.

Six months later, a union representative confronted me with an alleged customer complaint for mistreating the public. As someone who interviewed 200 people daily, it was impossible for me to remember everything. The threat of losing my job loomed over me, and I couldn't help but feel helpless.

It was then that I turned to Jesus for help. I began to pray about the situation, pouring my heart out to Him and asking Him to help me find a way out of this mess; and then something miraculous happened.

"NOTHING IS IMPOSSIBLE FOR JESUS," and He showed me the man's face and file, which I promptly forwarded to the union representative. As a result, the illegal alien was deported back to his country, and the very person who had previously threatened to fire me took credit for facilitating his exit. I couldn't believe it.

It was a true testament to the power of prayer and faith in God. At that moment, I realized that anything can be achieved through faith and trust in our Lord and Savior. It was a life-changing experience that I will never forget.

So, my message to you today is this, have faith in God's power and never underestimate what can be achieved through prayer. No matter how big or small your problems may seem, know that Jesus is with you every step of the way, ready to intervene and guide you toward a solution. Trust in Him, and you will see miracles happen in your life.

CHAPTER 14
SENIOR CITIZEN WANTED TO BE YOUNG

One morning, this elderly couple came into the Social Security Office seeking a replacement Medicare card. I was working at the front desk along with a co-worker. I asked the man, "How may I help you? He answered I need a replacement Medicare card." I completed the necessary computer forms and advised him that he would receive them in three weeks.

He began to leave, and I said, "Wait a minute, you're leaving your wife. The man said, "That old ass woman is not my wife; I have a young wife." I laughed, and the woman was hard of hearing and said, "Social Security must be paying you good money; you're so happy and laughing."

The couple then proceeded to amble towards the door, linked together hand in hand, a sight that warmed my heart. Whether the man's youthful spirit was contagious or perhaps it was just a testament to the power of love, seeing this elderly couple enjoying life to the fullest left me with a smile on my face for the rest of the day.

CHAPTER 15
THE DISOBEDIENT CHILD

Back in the day, children used to receive benefits while still attending high school. However, things turned unfavorable for a young girl who decided to play hooky and never obtained her diploma. Social Security soon caught wind of it and discovered that her mother had been overpaid a staggering $17,000.

I vividly remember my visit to their home, where I had to break the news to them. The poor mother was devastated and hurled insults at her daughter in a fit of anger. This situation had the potential to turn volatile, with threats of physical violence lingering in the air.

But even in the face of hostility, I remained calm and suggested that they accumulate their bills and work out an installment-based repayment plan. That way, they could pay what was affordable to them or write the whole thing off entirely.

However, these types of disputes can quickly turn into domestic squabbles where everyone is fighting over their share of the pie. Despite all of my efforts, in this particular case, repayment in installments was the only viable solution to settle the matter.

In all my years of experience, I have never witnessed a child so blatantly disrespect a parent. It was indeed a hard pill to swallow, but I remain optimistic that they will find a way to overcome this hurdle together, holding onto hope and love, the two most powerful forces known to mankind.

CHAPTER 16
DEFORMED CLAIMANT

As I sat at the front desk of the Social Security office, I couldn't help but feel the monotony of my job. Swipe ID, fill out forms, print out cards - repeat. It was as if I was running on autopilot. But then walked in a person who would change the course of my day.

He walked slowly up to the desk, and I asked for his identification, not looking up from my work. As I glanced down at his driver's license, I couldn't help but let out a chuckle. The picture was a mess - the man had undergone a severe injury to his neck that left him seeking aid from Social Security. I tried to hold in my laughter, but it was too late. The man responded, "What's so funny?" I looked up to apologize and realized that his appearance was even more startling than his license photo. His neck was twisted and jutted out to the side, causing his head to tilt uncomfortably. I better stop laughing before he beats my tail!

"I'm sorry," I said with a chuckle, "It's just that your photo is so... unfortunate." The man didn't seem to take offense, sensing my genuine sympathy. "Yeah, it's not exactly my best angle," he joked. "But it does the job."

I felt grateful for the encounter as he left the office with his new Social Security card. It was a reminder never to judge someone by their appearance. I may have laughed at first, but I left feeling enlightened and inspired by the resilience of the human spirit.

CHAPTER 17
I HURT MY BUTT ON THE FRONT DESK

As I strutted back from my lunch break in my fabulous heels, little did I know that disaster was just around the corner (or, rather, the front desk). My heel became entangled with a loose board underneath my stool, and I hurtled toward the ground. The next thing I knew, I had knocked myself unconscious!

I was saved by a co-worker with heart-shaped socks (of all things) who rushed to my aid. When I came to, I was met with the concerned faces of two elderly ladies - who looked like they belonged in a sitcom - hovering over me. As I slowly picked myself up off the floor, I couldn't help but notice that the entire office was laughing at my misfortune.

I struggled to sit comfortably for days, and everyone couldn't resist making fun of my unfortunate incident. Whenever I walked past, I heard snickers and whispers, "There goes Vanessa, who burst her ass on the front desk." Oh, the humiliation!

CHAPTER 18
THE DRUNK

As a Contract Representative with Social Security Administration, I met people from all walks of life, from training all world officials to enumerating all countries' citizens, ambassadors, and bank CEOs to the local drunk on the street. A drunk came into the office and told the Claim Representative. If you get me social security benefits, "I promise you I will drink no more than a FIFTH a day!" He was going to get toast every day.

While his offer may have been humorous, it made me reflect on the power these benefits have in the lives of many. It serves as a reminder of the Social Security Administration's significant role in providing a safety net for those in need.

Overall, working alongside people from different walks of life and hearing their unique stories has been a humbling experience. It has taught me to approach every interaction with empathy and compassion, recognizing that everyone has their own battles to fight.

CHAPTER 19
DEALING WITH EX CONVICTS

A person is not entitled to a social security retirement or disability payment since, while incarcerated, all their needs are met by taxpayer dollars. Prior to the change in the law, an ex-con visited the office per my request, seeking to recover from receiving an overpayment of $20,000 due to the change in the law.

I found out the beneficiary had spent the money, $20,000, on a 20-year-old car, and it failed. He continued to state how good prison was to him. I advised that he had to pay back the $20,000 he received, and he started pulling dead roaches off his clothes and throwing them at me. I screamed, and the guard led him out of the office.

The Field had to visit prisons to recover the overpayment under extenuating circumstances. He, the ex-con, was incapacitated for over 20 years for raping a woman to death after looking through the records.

Ultimately, the encounter left me uneasy and questioning the system's fairness. How could someone who had committed such a violent crime and expressed no remorse be entitled to the same benefits as law-abiding citizens? It was a question that continued to nag at me long after the incident was over.

It was wise of President Reagan during his era to stop prisoners from receiving Social Security benefits because the taxpayer dollars met all their needs.

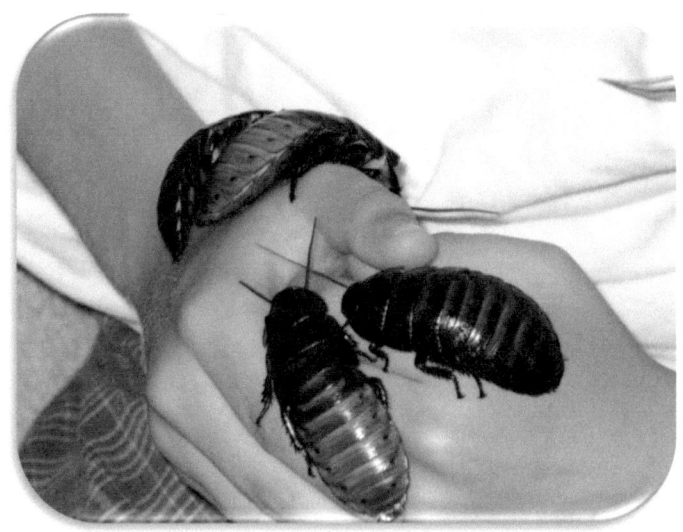

CHAPTER 20
A NOTE TO THE MILLENNIALS

Despite being a vital source of income for many retirees and elderly citizens, Social Security was never intended to be the sole means of financial support during retirement. Instead, its purpose is to provide a cushion for those who have aged and need assistance with basic living expenses. It is not designed to fully take care of an individual's financial needs, especially if they have significant medical expenses or other costs associated with aging.

In today's economy, relying solely on Social Security may not be enough to sustain a comfortable lifestyle in retirement. The rise of individual retirement accounts and plans such as the 401(k), Roth IRA, and Keough programs has made them increasingly popular among workers as a means of saving for retirement. However, these programs may not be sufficient to ensure financial security throughout an individual's retirement years.

In addition, withdrawing funds from a retirement account puts you in a higher tax bracket. Also, early withdrawals can be costly due to penalties and taxes. Your $500,000 retirement plan is now worth $300,000 or less. If you are under 59 1/2 years old, you are penalized. I remember I was going to take $25,000 before age and collected $16,900; the rest went to taxes and penalties. I was outdone! resulting in a significant reduction in the value of their retirement savings. This can be especially detrimental for those who may need to withdraw funds due to unforeseen circumstances.

Furthermore, even Social Security benefits are not exempt from taxes. Depending on the amount of income received from other sources, such as retirement accounts or investments, Social Security benefits may be subject to taxes depending on income from other sources, such as retirement income, investment income, or just from receiving Social Security retirement benefits of more than $25,000. This can further reduce the amount of income available for retirees to live on.

In conclusion, while Social Security and individual retirement plans can provide some measure of financial security during retirement, it is essential to plan ahead and have additional sources of income to support a comfortable lifestyle. It is crucial to seek the guidance of financial experts and take proactive measures to ensure financial stability in retirement.

CHAPTER 21
MY GIFT TO THE UNITED STATES CITIZENS

Here's my gift to US citizens: Alerts about possible deaths of social security beneficiaries without a death certificate. When investigating these cases, our office found that buying all those death certificates was too costly, and determining the state of death was difficult. As a result, my job was at stake.

I prayed for a solution, and God told me, "Use your Medicare records." I discovered that hospital and coroner records could also reveal dates of death. I found millions of deceased beneficiaries whose representative payees were all at one bank, and nobody had reported their deaths.

I used medical records to terminate these beneficiaries' benefits and collected $250,000. I shared my findings with the Integrity Department, and they collected another $250,000. This is one of the reasons why social security didn't go bankrupt twenty-two years ago.

I hope you enjoyed reading about my experiences at Social Security.

CHAPTER 22
AN INNOCENT GIRL

A neighbor of mine, Samantha, had always been close to her grandfather who had recently passed away. She had always thought she was one of the beneficiaries of his will, but she didn't know much more than that, as her grandfather had never discussed his estate with her. After his passing, Samantha was devastated but knew she needed to take care of his affairs.

Samantha soon found out that her grandfather's estate would need to go through probate before she could receive any inheritance. She had heard horror stories about probate and was not looking forward to the long and expensive process. However, she soon discovered that her grandfather had set up transfer-on-death designations on all of his bank accounts, leaving her as the beneficiary.

As a Social Security Administration officer, I advised Samantha to take the necessary steps to claim any Social Security payments her grandfather owed. This is benefits he did not cash while he was living. This is considered an underpayment of benefits and is payable to the estate or next of kin. I explained to her the process of filling out Form SSA-1724 and how gathering the necessary documentation would be important to ensure a smooth transaction.

I commend Samantha for taking the necessary steps to manage her grandfather's affairs during a difficult time. With careful planning and the right guidance, she was able to honor her grandfather's memory without any added stress or complications.

CHAPTER 23
HOW TO GET A CLAIM

Lost Funds: The Reality of Dormant Accounts

Whether a family member or not, if you have a checking or saving account with a balance, suddenly, it no longer exists. Contact the branch (Bank branch) secretary with the last statement or deposit book proving its existence. Normally before they forward the money or close the account, they contact the owner if they want to keep the account open or withdraw the funds. Normally after an account has no activities in a year, the bank closes the account and forwards the funds to the bank's headquarters state fund.

You must make a property claim with that state to release the funds to you. I remember I had a savings account with HEW for about $5,000. The bank branch was in Maryland, but HEW headquarters was in Washington, DC. The secretary gave me the address and telephone number of the property claim office in Washington, D.C. I filled in the necessary forms and received the funds. Most senior citizens have a nest egg for that day of departure. If you run across the books and have no revenue, take the necessary steps, starting with the branch secretary.

Remember, if you are in the same situation, start by contacting the branch secretary. It's never too late to retrieve lost funds and secure your future.

CHAPTER 24
COMPASSION

As a Contact Representative, demonstrating genuine empathy toward the public's needs is paramount. This includes individuals who may face mental disabilities while inhabiting an adult body but possess the mental capacity of a five-year-old. One particular instance comes to mind involving a lady in her thirties who would frequent our office on a daily basis. Despite the seemingly never-ending queues, she would patiently wait, her primary concern being the status of her check.

Being her primary point of contact, she would often approach me with the question, "Ms. Whatchamacallums, is my check coming next month?" These interactions allowed me to reassure her, putting her mind at ease. Given her unique circumstances, ensuring she felt heard and understood was crucial. Professionally and compassionately, I would offer the necessary reassurances, assuring her that her check was indeed on its way.

Our interactions with individuals like her reminded me of the importance of maintaining a professional tone and approach. Despite the challenges they may face, it is our duty to treat them with the utmost respect and dignity. By embodying the role of Ms. Whatchamacallums, I was able to contribute to creating a welcoming and supportive environment for all individuals who sought assistance from our office.

Expanding on this experience, it serves as a powerful reminder of the significance of empathy and understanding in our line of work. Each day presents new opportunities to positively impact the lives of those we serve, even through seemingly small acts of reassurance and support. As a Contact Representative, it is imperative to approach each interaction with professionalism, compassion, and the willingness to go the extra mile for those in need.

CHAPTER 25
HELPED ALL MANKIND BUT COULD NOT HELP MY FATHER

My father worked from the age of seven until he was seventy. His lifelong dream was to retire and receive social security benefits. Unfortunately, his father passed away when he was only two years old, and his mother died when he was seven. A kind neighbor took him in but put him to work caring for lumber at the sawmill. Due to this, my father only received a first-grade education, where he could only read three-letter words and count.

Despite these adversities, my father overcame these obstacles and opened a trash removal business. Being self-employed means, one has to pay for half of all employees' retirements, along with their own. When my father turned sixty-five, he filed for retirement only to learn that the law states one must sell and liquidate their business or have nothing to do with it to receive 43 benefits. As my father was still holding the business for his children, who wished to own it one day, he had no choice but to wait until he turned seventy to receive benefits.

Sadly, my father passed away on his seventieth birthday, never receiving a dime from Social Security. Although I could help everyone, I could not help my father, the man who carried trash on his back and reared me.

CHAPTER 26
THE CANCER VICTIM

A lady came to me with a notice, expressing her astonishment about being overpaid an astounding $20,000 due to a miscalculation of her benefits. However, her account didn't end there. She went on to share a remarkable story of resilience and trust in a higher power. It turns out that when she initially received the unexpected windfall, she also received devastating news from her doctor - she had just six months left to live. Rather than succumbing to despair, she embraced life with unwavering faith and determination.

With the newfound funds, she embarked on a journey of fulfilling her heart's desires. She seized the opportunity to create unforgettable memories and experiences. From purchasing a mobile home that she could call her own to meticulously furnishing it with every comfort imaginable, she spared no expense in making her dream a reality. But her aspirations didn't stop there.

She adorned herself with the finest clothes, treating herself to a wardrobe befitting her newfound zest for life. And, of course, she acquired a car, enabling her to explore the world that lay beyond her doorstep.

Throughout her journey, the lady emphasized the power of God, firmly believing that the doctors' predictions were not the final word. And remarkably, against all odds, those six months turned into two decades of beautiful, vibrant life. As she sat before me, she proudly presented a stack of bills, representing the countless adventures and blessings she had encountered along the way. It was a testament to her indomitable spirit and unwavering faith.

Moved by her story, I offered her my guidance. I assured her I would do everything in my power to assist her in managing and eventually paying off those bills. Together, we would navigate this journey of financial responsibility, acknowledging her incredible strength in the face of adversity. As we took the first steps towards finding a solution, her story continued to serve as an inspiration - a reminder that with faith and determination, we can overcome any obstacle that comes our way.

CHAPTER 27
THE LITTLE GIRL WHO FOUND HOPE

A young lady came into the office to return her father's check because he had died from AIDS. She was a young girl, about 17 years old. She sat at my desk crying, pouring her out to me, stating everyone was pointing at her and staying far because her father had AIDS. Mind you; this was the early nineties when AIDS first came out. She said he had her before he became gay, and she did not have Aids. She said she was heartbroken. I told her Honey, you need to get away and have a new beginning. I told her about a book I found in the library called Organizations of Associations, giving away grant money in any field you want to study. The only requirement was to work for the company two years after your degree or certification.

    She returned, telling me I have a new start in life because of you. I received a scholarship to attend a school in Pennsylvania. I think it was an acting school or of the Arts. I remember her saying it was college. She thanked me, and I said look at God. Mending the broken heart.

CHAPTER 28
THE MAN WHO HAD NO TEETH

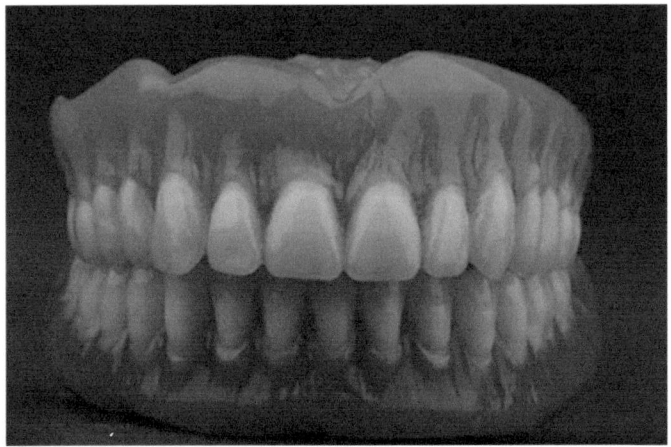

I received a heartfelt phone call from a senior citizen who was clearly upset about his dental situation. His voice was filled with disappointment as he asked me, "Miss, does social security pay for dental work?" The man said the dog ate my teeth"! My heart sank as he explained that his mischievous dog had devoured his teeth. It was a difficult situation, and unfortunately, back then, many seniors suffered from dental problems and were in dire need of dental work.

With empathy in my voice, I advised the caller that Medicare did not cover dental work during that time. I couldn't help but imagine how devastating it must have been for him, unable to enjoy his meals properly. However, I assured him that there might be other avenues for assistance. While I didn't have firsthand knowledge of an organization that could help, I mentioned that social services did step in to offer support in certain cases.

But the times have changed, and I wanted to offer him a glimmer of hope. Nowadays, Medicare covers dental work, vision, and prescription medications for an additional premium. It's a remarkable shift that brings relief and empowerment to seniors who deserve nothing but the best in their golden years.

He asked how much it would cost for the prescription, and I answered an additional $1,000 a month. What??? The average check is around $1,825. What do you have to live on?

In conclusion, this conversation with the senior citizen made me realize the significance of advocating for accessible healthcare for everyone, especially our aging population. Medicare's expansion to include dental work is truly inspirational, as it ensures that our seniors can continue to enjoy their meals, maintain their oral health, and ultimately live their lives to the fullest. Let us celebrate this positive change and continue working towards a society where affordable healthcare is a basic right for all.

CHAPTER 29
THE PROPHESY

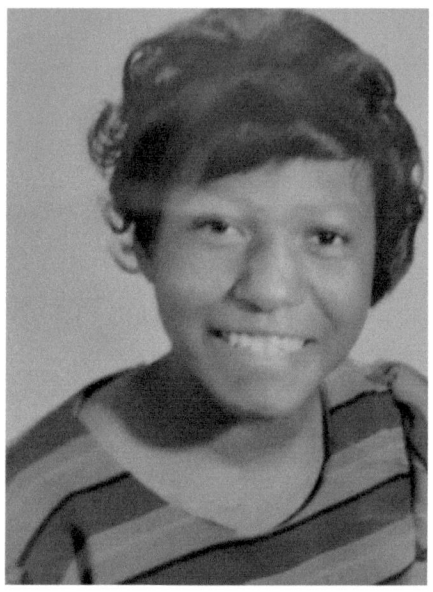

In my early twenties, I was seeking to buy this duplex house. It was cute but unknowingly had a lot of work to be done, and it was in an undesirable neighborhood. Young, I did not know that you bought the neighborhood at the time. The underwriter stated, "Your degree is in accounting; why are you working for Social Security? I am going to ask you to write an essay, why are you working for Social Security?" I said to myself, "A dumb question; I'm going to give them a dumb answer." I wrote the essay and advised them that with my degree, maybe one day, I would come up with a solution to keep Social Security from going broke.

Little did I know that this seemingly trivial moment would become a turning point in my life. The underwriter's question had ignited a fire within me - a determination to make a difference in the world through my work at Social Security.

In my essay, I conveyed my deep belief that my accounting background would play a crucial role in finding a solution to the challenges facing Social Security. I explained that with my degree, I would strive to develop innovative methods to ensure this vital system remains sustainable for future generations. It was a bold proclamation, but I knew I had the skills and determination to back it up.

The story doesn't end there. As fate would have it, the mortgage company granted me the opportunity to purchase my own home. This achievement was particularly meaningful for a young, single, black girl with soaring aspirations. It served as a reminder that no dream is too big or too far out of reach.

Reflecting on this experience, I realized the profound truth hidden within. The moral of the story is that we have the power to speak things into existence. By boldly asserting our goals and aspirations, we can attract opportunities that propel us toward success. In the case of Social Security, my determination and belief in finding a solution led me ultimately to a path where I could make a meaningful difference.

CHAPTER 30
IS SOCIAL SECURITY GOING BROKE?

"The proof is in the pudding"
"The proof is in the figures"
"Check out my calculation"
"Now you make the decision: is it going broke?"

There are about 331.9 million people in the United States. Seventy-Six percent of the population pays social security taxes. 76 percent of 331.9 million equals 252,244,000 people paying taxes. The tax people pay is 6.2 percent of their wages. Their employee pays another 6.2 percent of wages, or half, until they reach a limit of $160,200 in wages. The average income in the United States is $56,000 a year. My figure is based on an average salary of $56,000 a year.

The Employer pays: $3,472.00

Employee: $3,472.00

Total Taxes paid: $6,944.00

The Total per person paying:	$252,244,000
X	$6,944
Total Revenue	$1,751,582,336,000
Social Sec. benefits paid out in a year	$1,000,000,000,000
Profit	$751,582,336,000

The Social Security Funds should only be applied for what they are specified for: the beneficiaries. Instead of paying other funds as needed. The surplus should be placed in an annuity. With the false prediction that it would be broke by 2035, my calculations say that if we saved the surplus for 12 years, we would have at least $9,018,988,032,000.

Don't let your hard-earned money go to waste! Start questioning where your social security contributions are going and make sure the government is using those funds for the benefit of those who truly need them. Remember, your future depends on it!

Courtesy of: https://www.ssa.gov/news/press/factsheets/basicfact-alt.pdf

Fact Sheet
SOCIAL SECURITY

In 2023, an average of almost 67 million Americans per month will receive a Social Security benefit, totaling over one trillion dollars in benefits paid during the year.

Snapshot of a Month: December 2022 Beneficiary Data

- Retired workers   48.6 million $88.7 billion $1,825 average monthly benefit
  - dependents   2.7 million $2.4 billion
- Disabled workers   7.6 million $11.3 billion $1,483 average monthly benefit
  - dependents   1.2 million $0.6 billion
- Survivors   5.9 million $8.5 billion

Social Security is the major source of income for most of the elderly.
- Nearly nine out of ten people age 65 and older were receiving a Social Security benefit as of December 31, 2022.
- Social Security benefits represent about 30% of the income of the elderly. *
- Among elderly Social Security beneficiaries, 37% of men and 42% of women receive 50% or more of their income from Social Security. *
- Among elderly Social Security beneficiaries, 12% of men and 15% of women rely on Social Security for 90% or more of their income. *

*This information is from research released in 2021 using 2015 data. See this link for more information

Social Security provides more than just retirement benefits.
- Retired workers and their dependents accounted for 76.9% of total benefits paid in 2022.
- Disabled workers and their dependents accounted for 11.6% of total benefits paid in 2022.
  - About 90 percent of workers aged 21-64 in covered employment in 2022 and their families have protection in the event of a severe and prolonged disability.
  - About 1 in 4 of today's 20 year-olds will become disabled before reaching age 67.
  - 65% of the private sector workforce has no long-term disability insurance.
- Survivors of deceased workers accounted for 11.5% of total benefits paid in 2022.
  - More than one in eight of today's 20-year-olds will die before reaching age 67.
  - About 97% of persons aged 20-49 who worked in covered employment in 2022 have survivors insurance protection for their children under age 18 (and surviving spouses caring for children under age 16).

An estimated 183 million workers will work in OASDI-covered employment in 2023.
- 31% of the workforce in private industry has no access to private pension coverage.
- About two-thirds (63%) of workers report they are currently saving for retirement. Having an employer-sponsored retirement savings plan is a key factor in whether Americans save for retirement. Only 16% of those without access to an employer-sponsored plan said they have any retirement savings.

➢ In 1940, the life expectancy of a 65-year-old was almost 14 years; today it is over 20 years.

➢ The number of Americans 65 and older will increase from about 58 million in 2022 to about 76 million by 2035. [1]

➢ In 2022, there are an estimated 2.8 covered workers per each Social Security beneficiary. By 2035, the Trustees estimate there will be 2.3 covered workers for each beneficiary.

Do they know, or they just don't know?

They're supposed to have gone broke.

Who is deceiving the people?

Satan is a liar. The devil is busy, but

GOD IS STILL ON THE THRONE!!!

ABOUT THE AUTHOR

I started as a Cooperative Education business major at DuVal Senior High School. I worked as a bookkeeper at the Citizen Bank of Maryland during my senior high school year.

After I graduated from DuVal, I attended Prince George's Community College, where I received an Associated Arts Degree in Accounting. My degree was useful in Private Industry and Government jobs. In 1977, I took the government entrance examination scoring 105, when 70 points were only needed for a position. The Federal Government was calling me for positions for a Federal Government job.

My first job with Federal Government was aiding FBI agents and Administration Law Judges with Dishonorable Soldiers' Court Cases. Later became an Advocate for Social Security, SSI, and Medicare beneficiaries with the Social Security Administration. Currently, I'm a certified minority business owner for one of the largest certified minority-owned trash businesses in the United States of America.

Imagine a journey of hard work, dedication, and determination that led to a fulfilling career in government service and ownership of a thriving business. As a powerful advocate for Social Security beneficiaries, I easily interpreted complex laws and regulations, ensuring those in need received the help they deserved. After years of public service, I took my talents into the private sector, becoming a certified minority business owner that served the D.C. and Metropolitan Illustrious community.

Step into the world of our lives—a world filled with challenges, struggles, and triumphs—and be inspired by the incredible journey of an exceptional woman.

Printed by Libri Plureos GmbH in Hamburg, Germany